Disney

THE LION KING

MUSIC FROM THE MOTION PICTURE SOUNDTRACK

ISBN 978-1-5400-6752-4

Visit Hal Leonard Online at
www.halleonard.com

Contact us:
Hal Leonard
7777 West Bluemound Road
Milwaukee, WI 53213
Email: info@halleonard.com

In Europe, contact:
Hal Leonard Europe Limited
42 Wigmore Street
Marylebone, London, W1U 2RN
Email: info@halleonardeurope.com

In Australia, contact:
Hal Leonard Australia Pty. Ltd.
4 Lentara Court
Cheltenham, Victoria, 3192 Australia
Email: info@halleonard.com.au

BATTLE FOR PRIDE ROCK

Composed by
HANS ZIMMER

Moderately slow, expressively

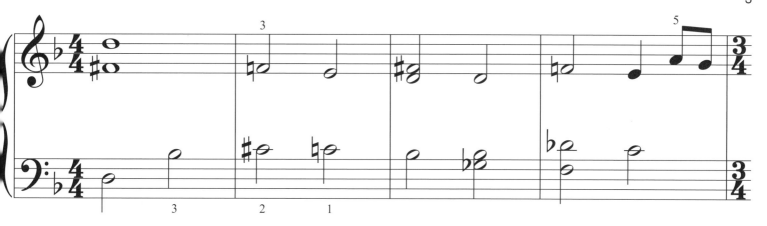

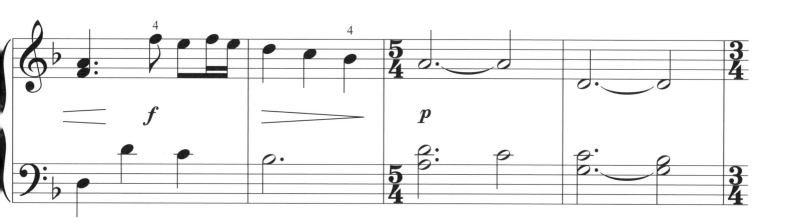

Moderately

4

Slowly, steadily

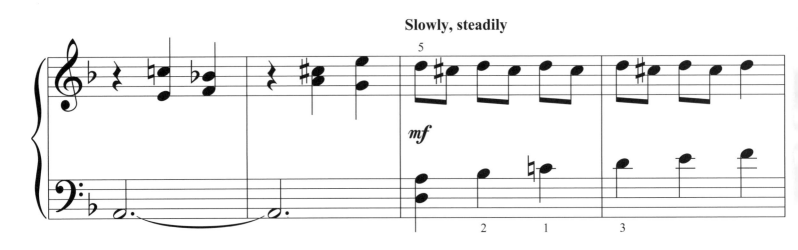

Moderately slow

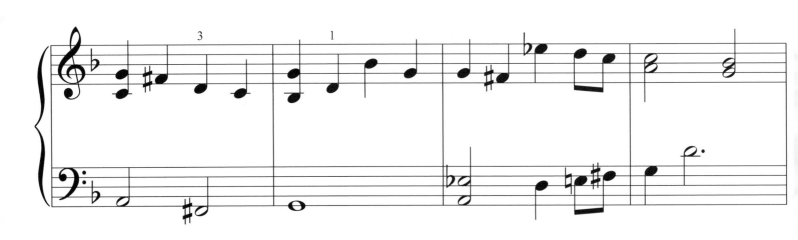

Quickly, in 2

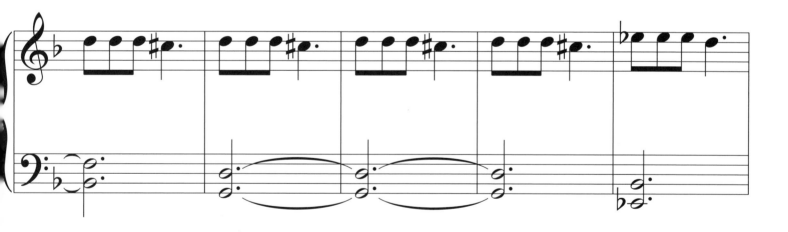

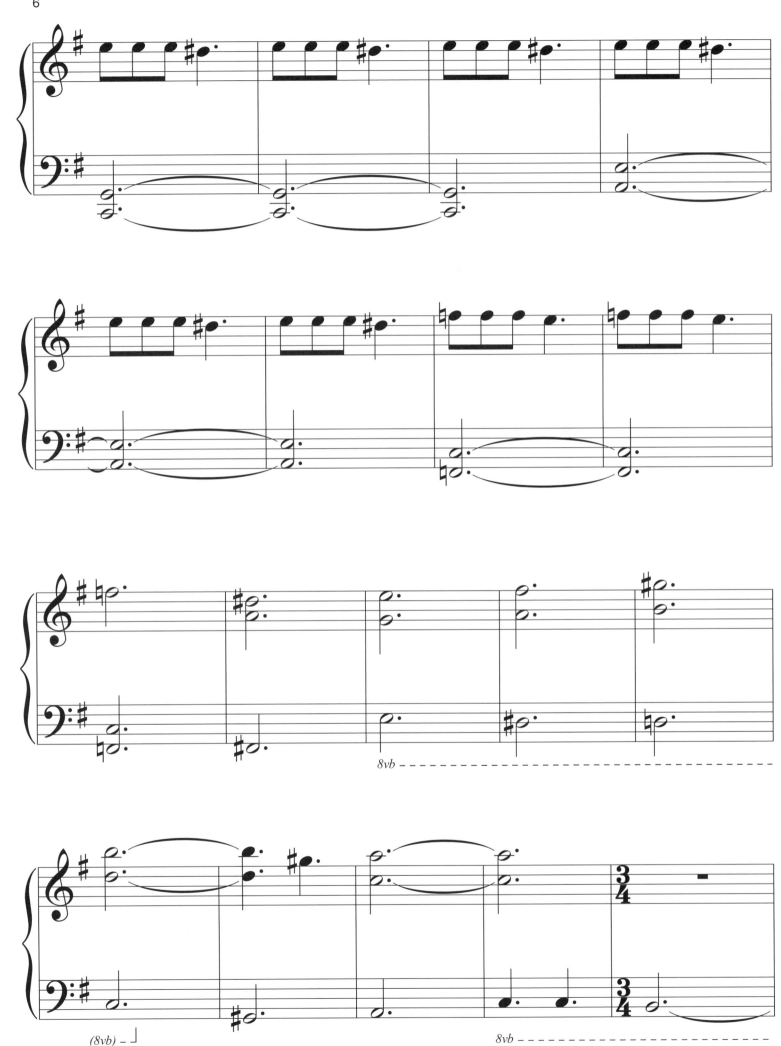

Moderately slow

(8vb)

Majestically

CAN YOU FEEL THE LOVE TONIGHT

Music by ELTON JOHN
Lyrics by TIM RICE

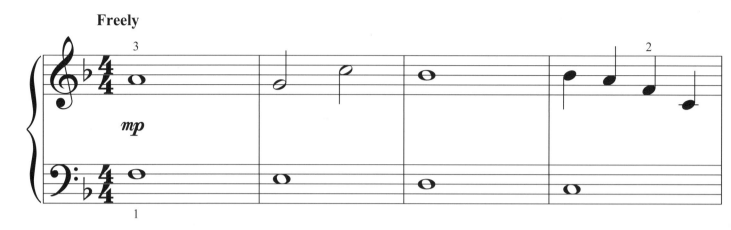

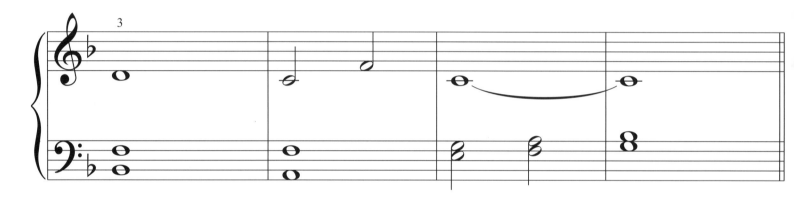

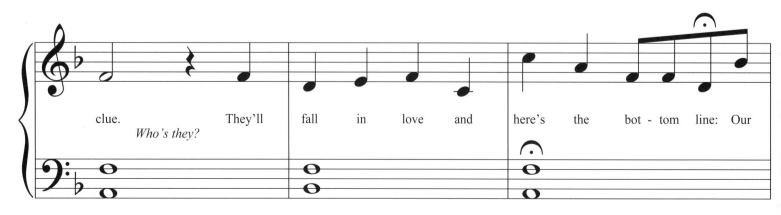

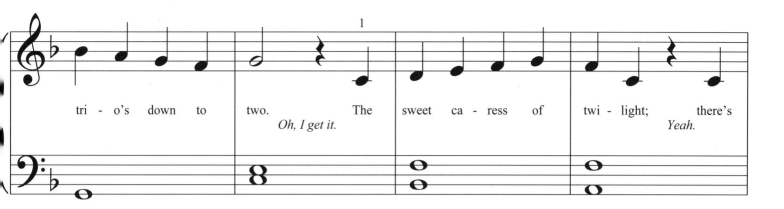

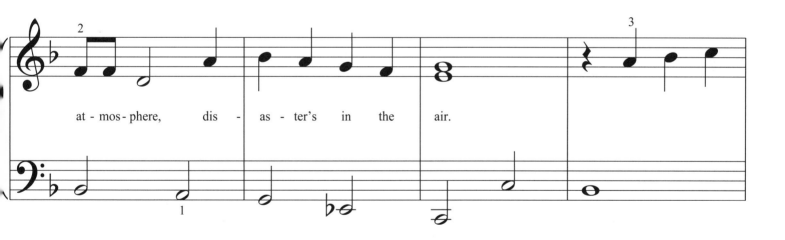

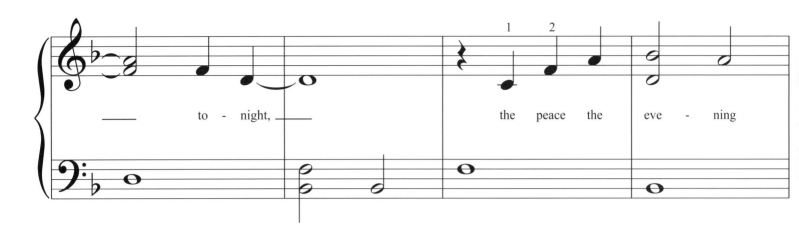

to - night, _____ the peace the eve - ning

brings? _____ The world, for once, _____ in

per - fect har - mo - ny with all its liv - ing things. ___

SIMBA:

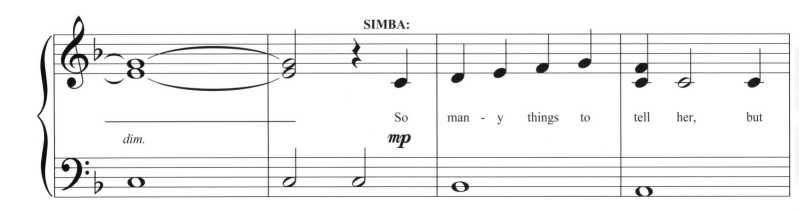

dim. **mp** So man - y things to tell her, but

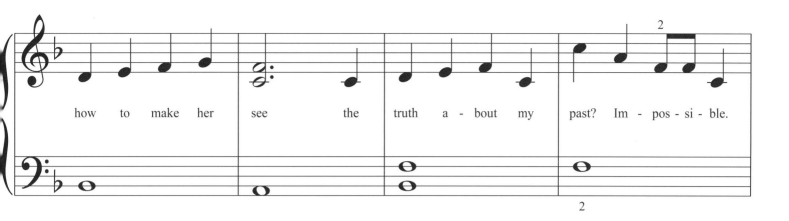

how to make her see the truth a - bout my past? Im - pos - si - ble.

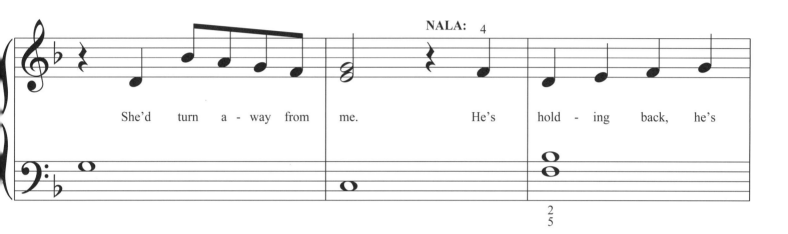

NALA:

She'd turn a - way from me. He's hold - ing back, he's

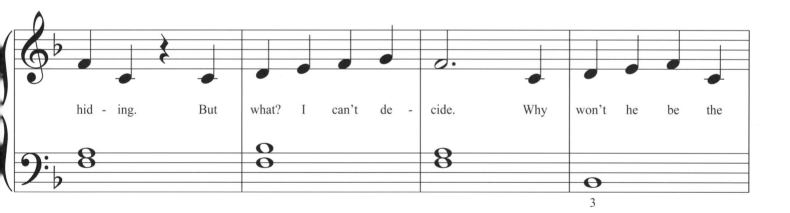

hid - ing. But what? I can't de - cide. Why won't he be the

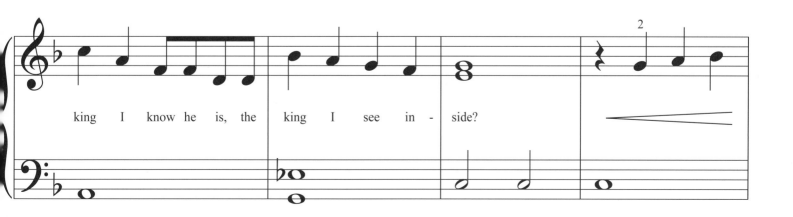

king I know he is, the king I see in - side?

NALA & SIMBA:

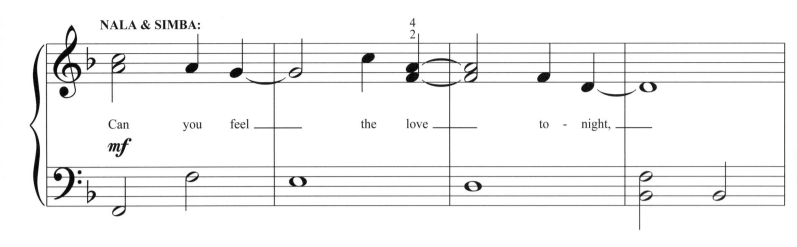

Can you feel _____ the love _____ to - night, _____

mf

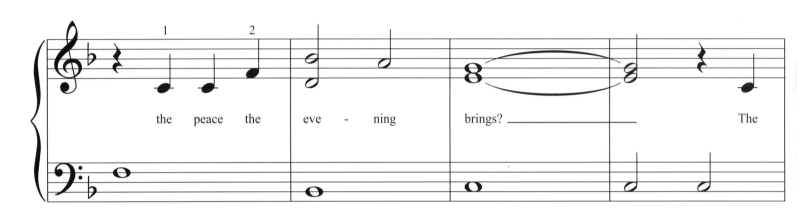

the peace the eve - ning brings? _____ The

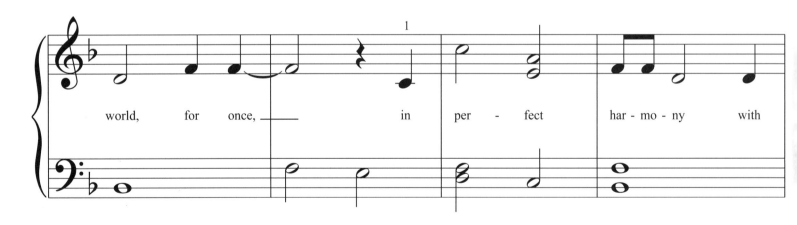

world, for once, _____ in per - fect har - mo - ny with

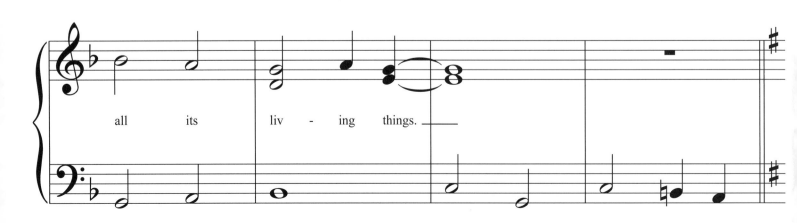

all its liv - ing things. _____

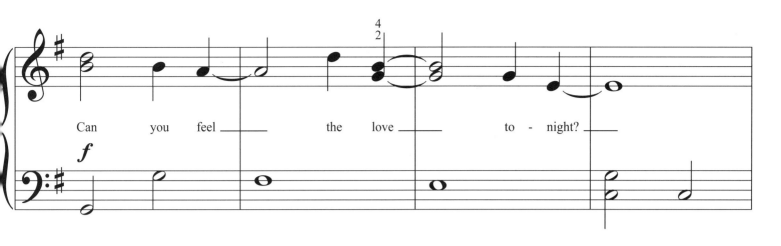

Can you feel ____ the love ____ to - night? ____

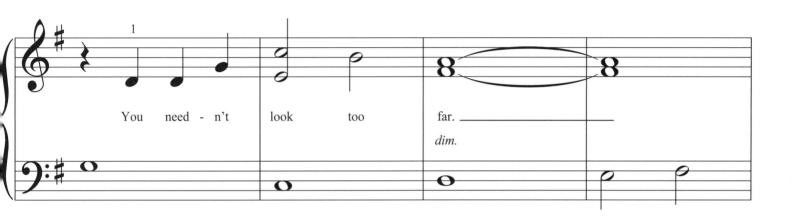

You need - n't look too far. _____

Steal - ing through the night's un - cer - tain - ties,

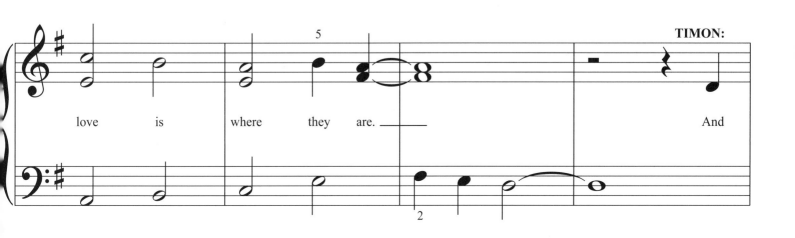

love is where they are. ____ And

TIMON:

if he falls in love _____ to - night, _____

mp

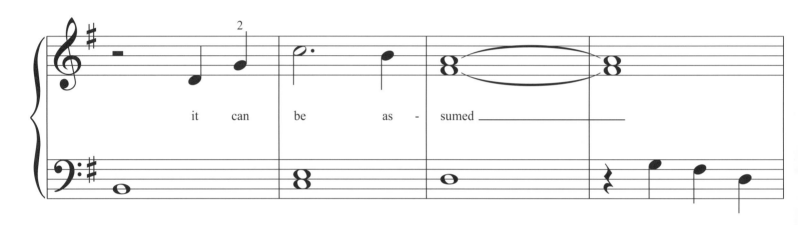

it can be as - sumed _____

PUMBAA: **TIMON & PUMBAA:**

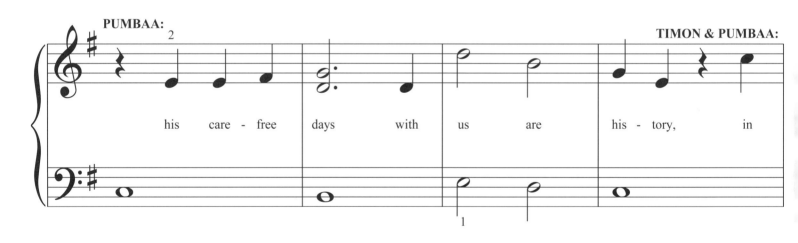

his care - free days with us are his - tory, in

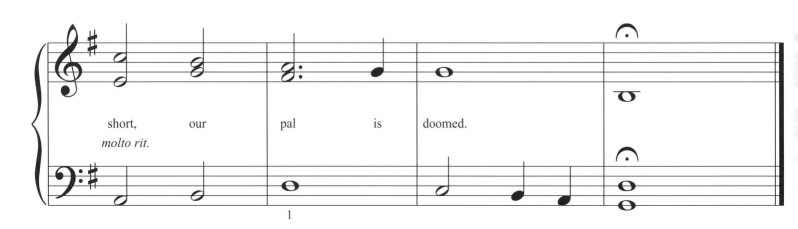

short, our pal is doomed.

molto rit.

CIRCLE OF LIFE/NANTS' INGONYAMA

NANTS' INGONYAMA
Music and Lyrics by HANS ZIMMER
and LEBOHANG MORAKE

Moderately

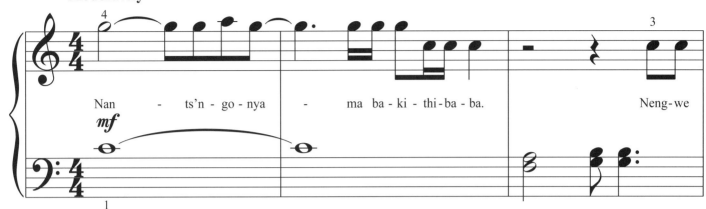

Nan - ts'n - go - nya - ma ba - ki - thi - ba - ba. Neng-we

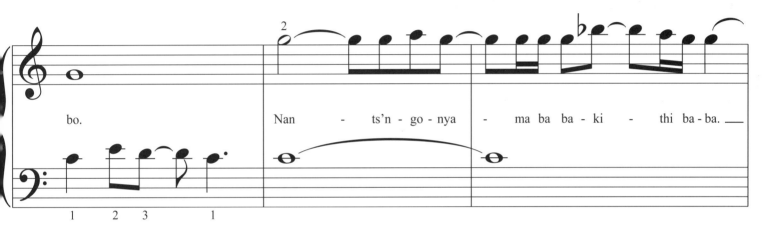

bo. Nan - ts'n - go - nya - ma ba ba - ki - thi ba - ba.

Neng - we - ba. He le le si - zo ngco ba - ba - ba.

I - ngo-nya - ma neng - we na - ma ba - la. I - ngo-nya - ma neng - we na - ma ba - la.

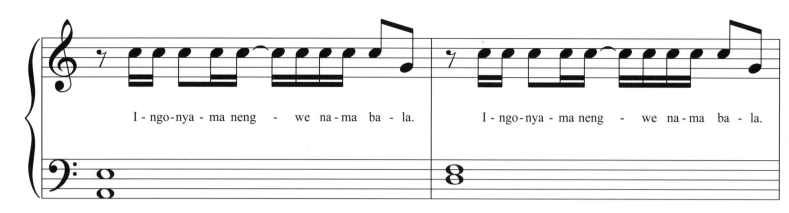

I - ngo-nya - ma neng — we na - ma ba - la.   I - ngo-nya - ma neng — we na - ma ba - la.

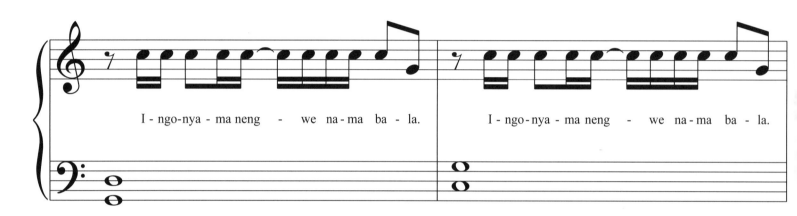

I - ngo-nya - ma neng — we na-ma ba - la.   I - ngo-nya - ma neng — we na-ma ba - la.

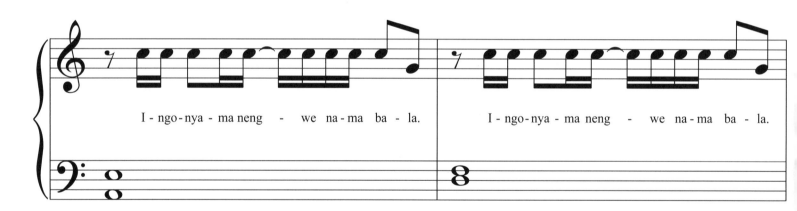

I - ngo-nya - ma neng — we na-ma ba - la.   I - ngo-nya - ma neng — we na-ma ba - la.

CIRCLE OF LIFE
Music by ELTON JOHN
Lyrics by TIM RICE

From the   day we ar - rive ____ on the plan - et _____ and

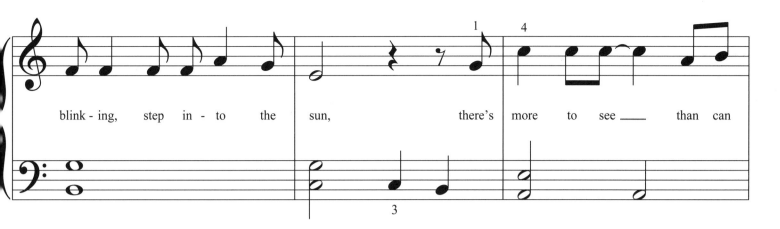

blink - ing, step in - to the sun, there's more to see _____ than can

ev - er be seen, _____ more to do than can ev - er be done. There's

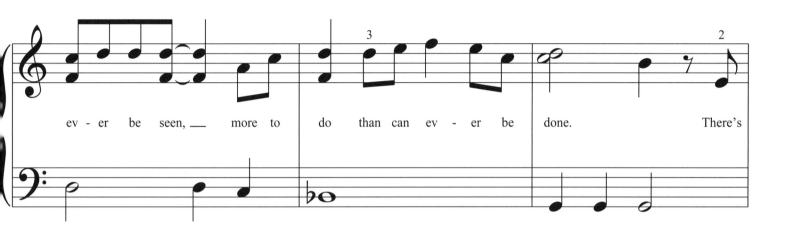

far too much _____ to take in _____ here, more to find than can ev - er be

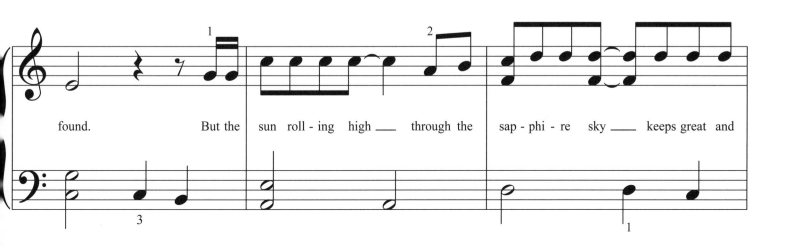

found. But the sun roll - ing high _____ through the sap - phi - re sky _____ keeps great and

small on the end - less round.___ It's the cir - cle of life,

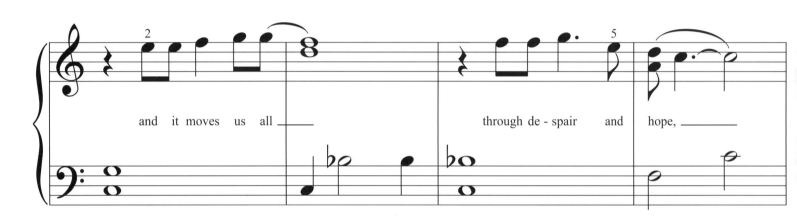

and it moves us all ___ through de - spair and hope, ___

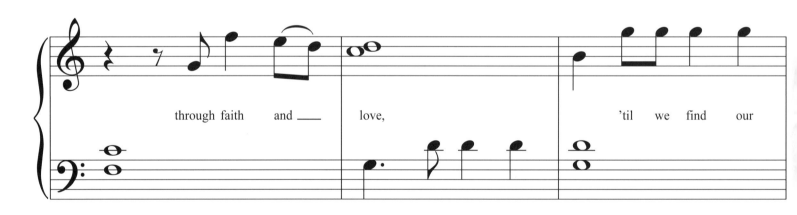

through faith and ___ love, 'til we find our

place ___ on the path un - wind - ing

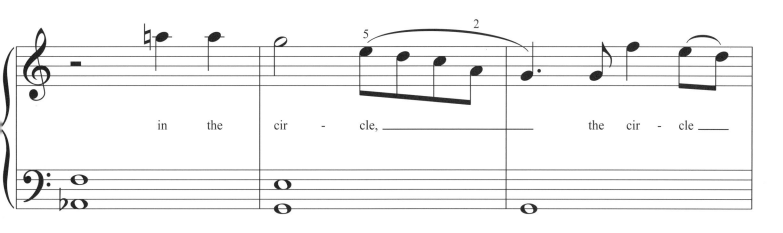

in the cir - cle, _____ the cir - cle ____

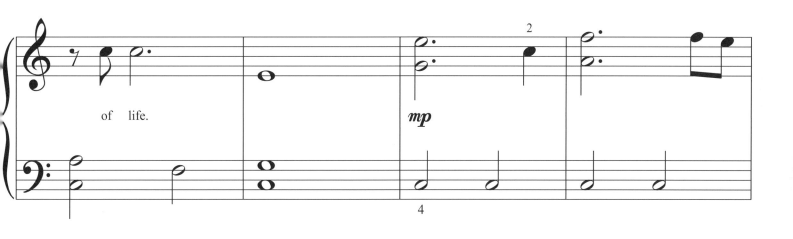

of life.

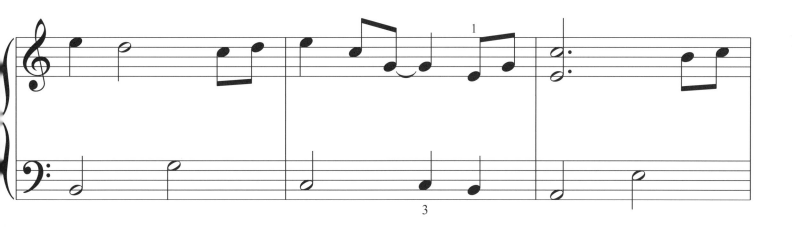

It's the cir - cle of life,

f

and it moves us all _____

through de - spair and

hope, _____ through faith and ___ love,

'til we find our place _____ on the path un -

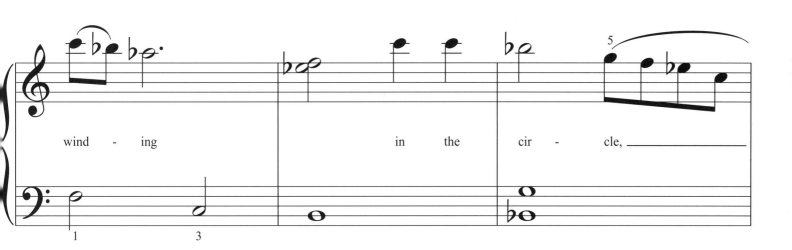

wind - ing in the cir - cle, _____

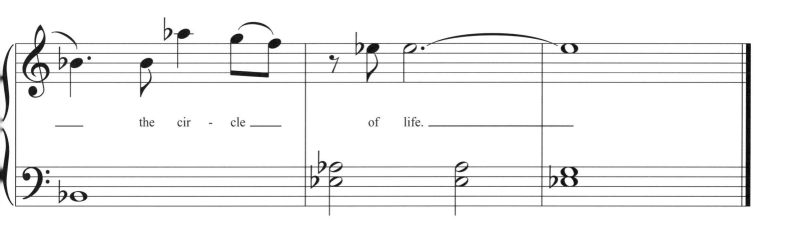

___ the cir - cle ___ of life. _____

HAKUNA MATATA

Music by ELTON JOHN
Lyrics by TIM RICE

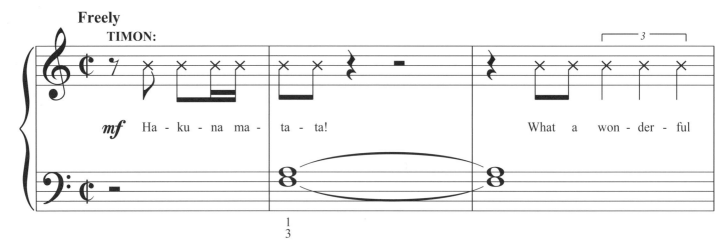

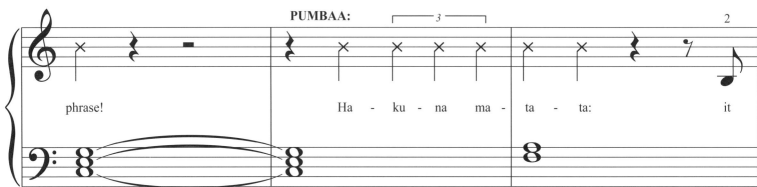

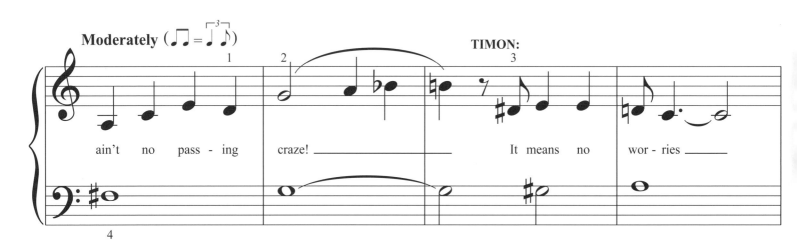

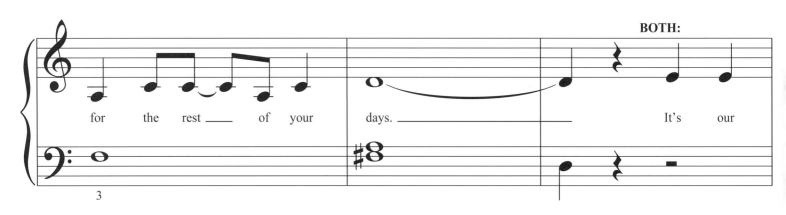

23

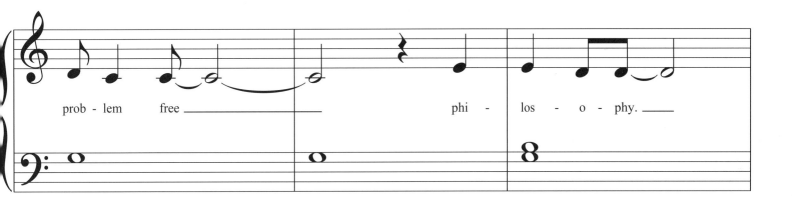

prob - lem free _____ _____ phi - los - o - phy. _____

TIMON:

Ha - ku - na ma - ta - ta.

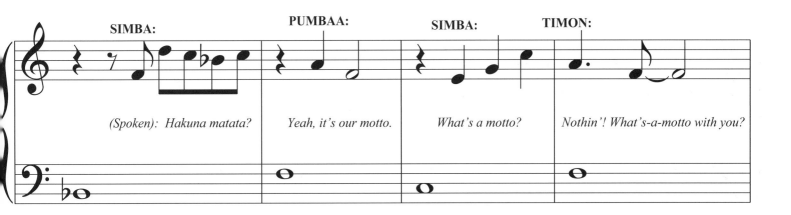

SIMBA: (Spoken): Hakuna matata?

PUMBAA: Yeah, it's our motto.

SIMBA: What's a motto?

TIMON: Nothin'! What's-a-motto with you?

PUMBAA: Nice! Boom!

Those two words will solve all your problems.

TIMON: Yeah.

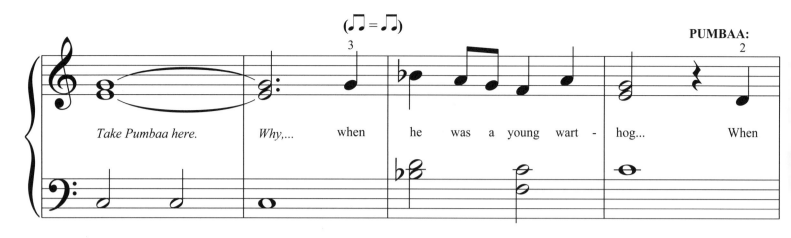

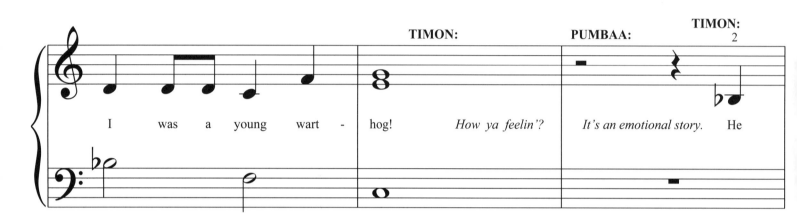

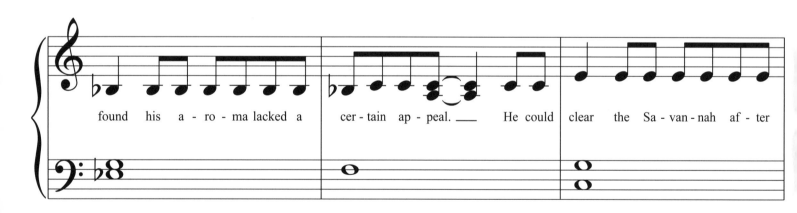

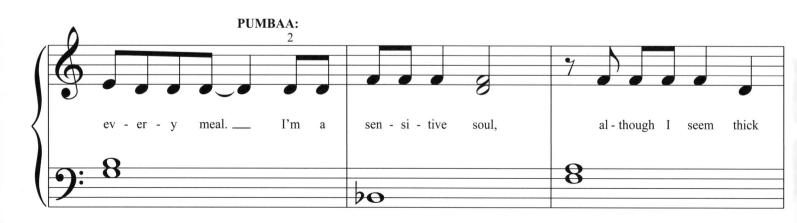

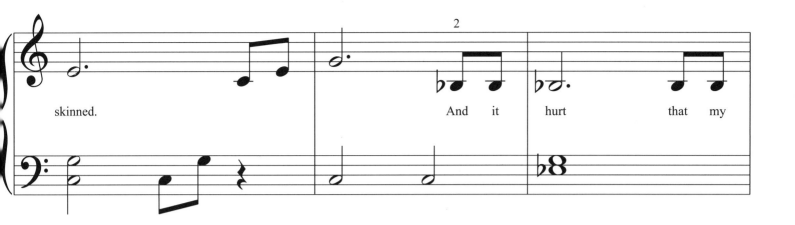

skinned.　　　　　　　　　　And　it　　hurt　　　that　my

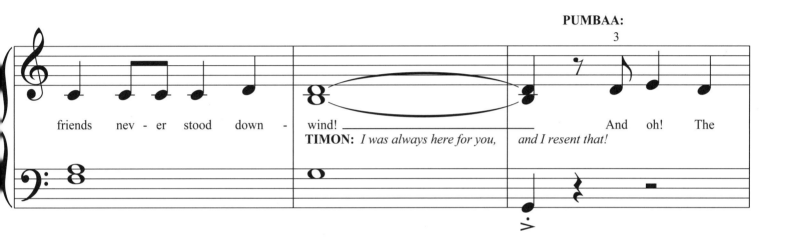

PUMBAA:

friends　nev - er　stood　down - wind! _____　　　　And　oh!　The

TIMON: *I was always here for you,*　*and I resent that!*

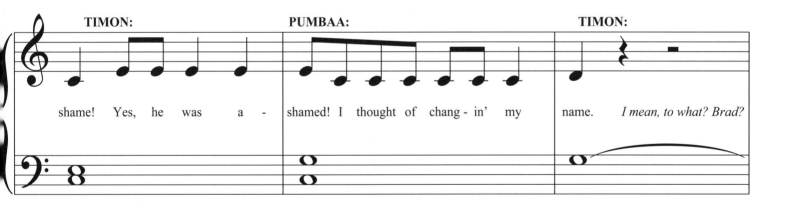

TIMON:　　　　　　　　**PUMBAA:**　　　　　　　　**TIMON:**

shame!　Yes,　he　was　a - shamed!　I　thought　of　chang - in'　my　name.　　*I mean, to what? Brad?*

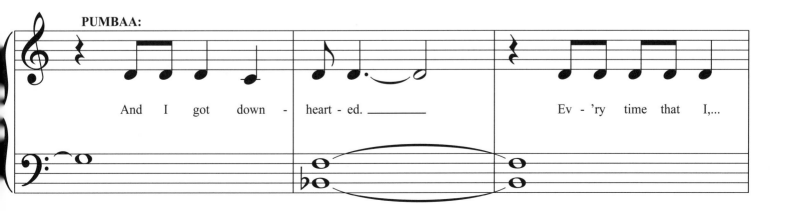

PUMBAA:

And　I　got　down - heart - ed. _____　　　　Ev - 'ry　time　that　I,...

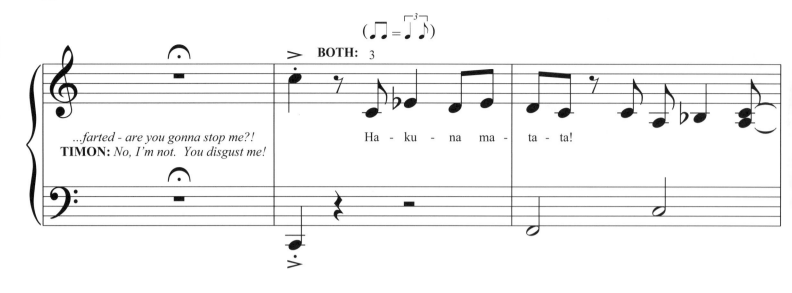

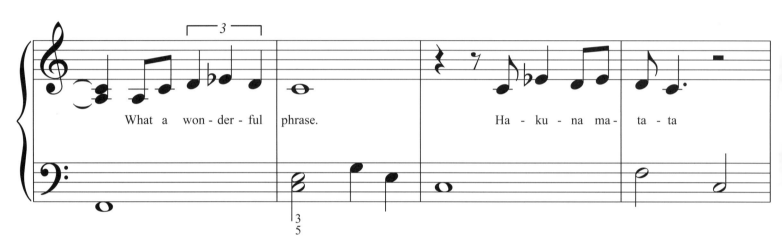

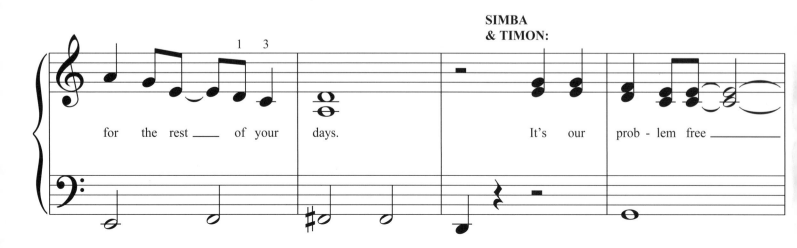

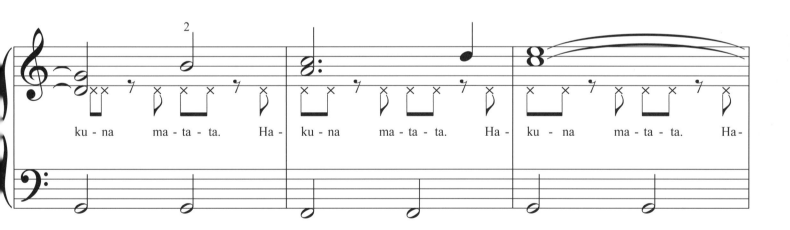

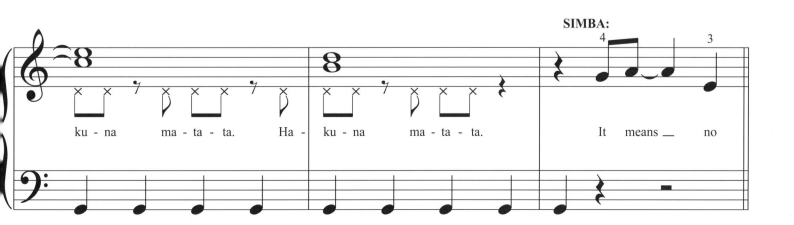

wor - ries _____ for the rest _____ of your days.

ALL:

It's our prob - lem free _____ phi -

SIMBA:

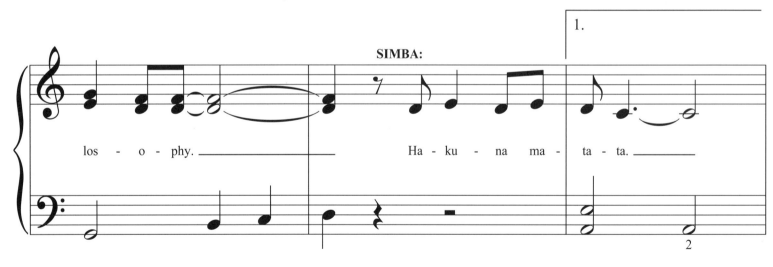

los - o - phy. _____ Ha - ku - na ma - ta - ta. _____

1.
2.

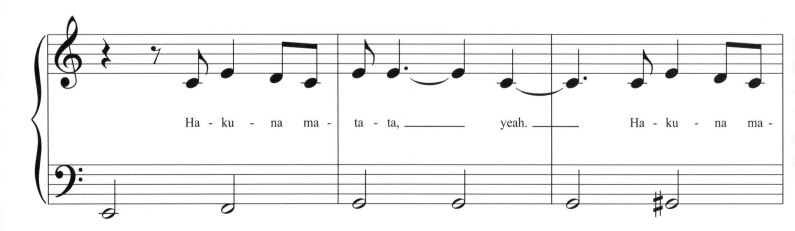

Ha - ku - na ma - ta - ta, _____ yeah. _____ Ha - ku - na ma -

HE LIVES IN YOU

Music and Lyrics by MARK MANCINA,
JAY RIFKIN and LEBOHANG MORAKE

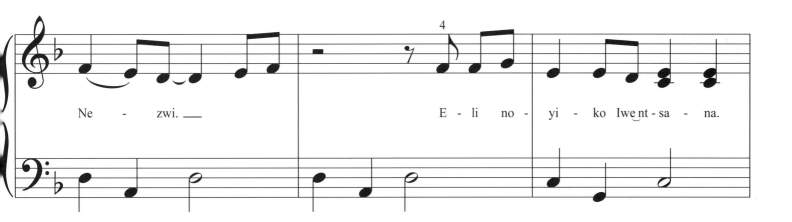

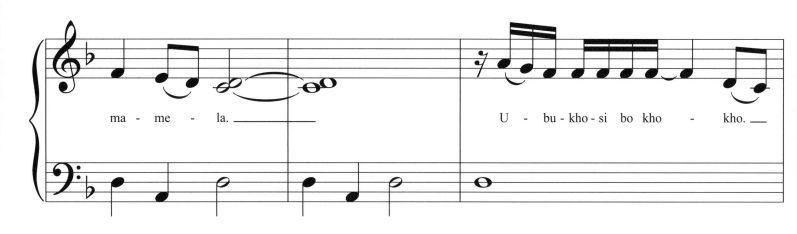

ma - me - la. _____ U - bu - kho - si bo kho - kho. _____

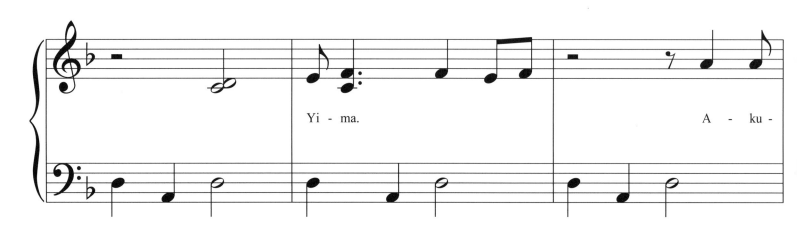

Yi - ma. A - ku -

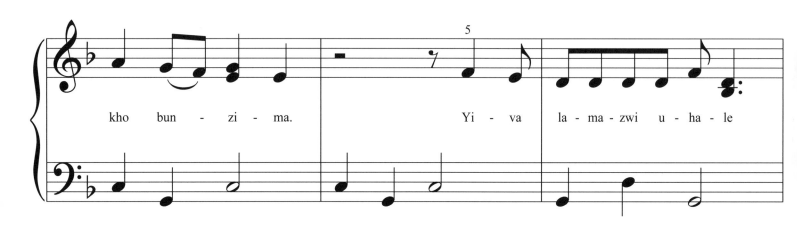

kho bun - zi - ma. Yi - va la - ma - zwi u - ha - le

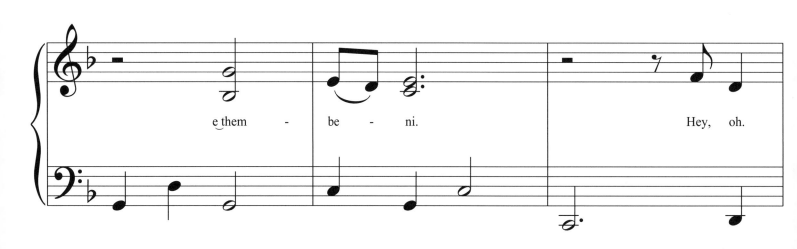

e them - be - ni. Hey, oh.

na - yo. Nan - sene - man - zi - ni,

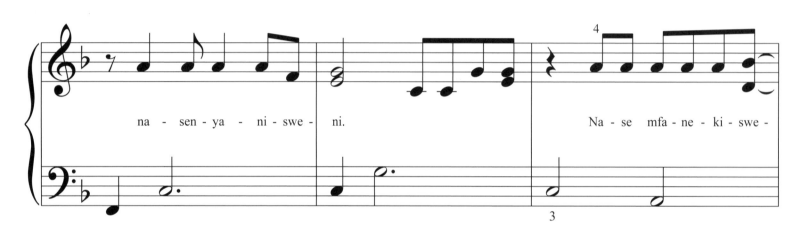

na - sen - ya - ni - swe - ni. Na - se mfa - ne - ki - swe -

- ni wa - kho. U - phi - la ku - we.

To Coda

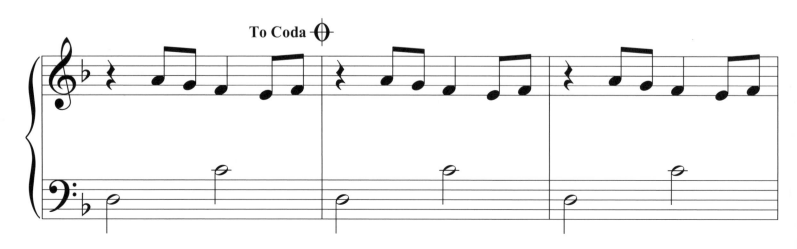

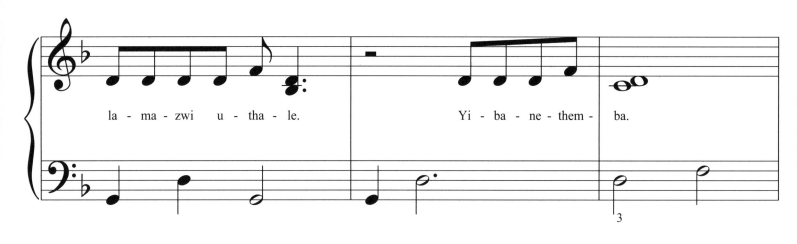

la - ma - zwi u - tha - le.   Yi - ba - ne - them - ba.

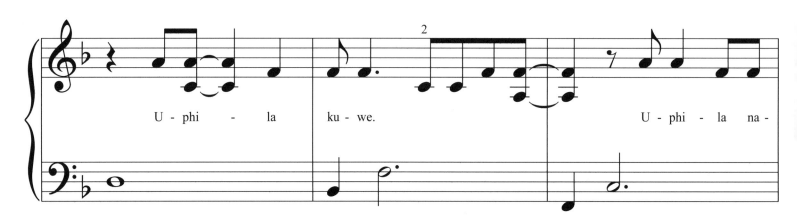

U - phi - la   ku - we.   U - phi - la na -

kum.   U - hla - l'e - jon - gi - le.

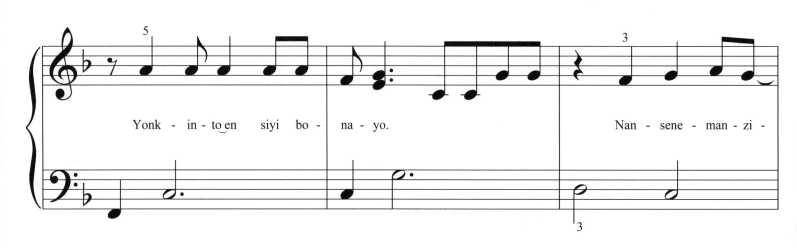

Yonk - in - to en siyi bo - na - yo.   Nan - sene - man - zi -

- ni,   na - sen - ya - ni - swe - ni.

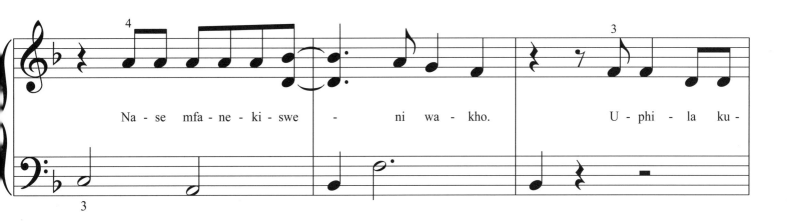

Na - se mfa - ne - ki - swe - ni wa - kho.   U - phi - la ku -

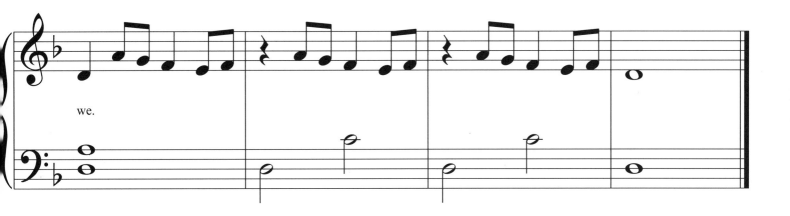

we.

English Translation

Here is a lion and a striped tiger.
Night and the spirit of life, calling. Listen.
And a voice, with the fear of a child, answers. Listen.
Throne of the ancestors.
Wait. There's no mountain too great.
Hear these words and have faith. Have faith.
Hey, listen.
He lives in you. He lives in me.
He watches over everything we see.
Into the water, into the truth,
In your reflection, he lives in you.
He lives in you.

I JUST CAN'T WAIT TO BE KING

Music by ELTON JOHN
Lyrics by TIM RICE

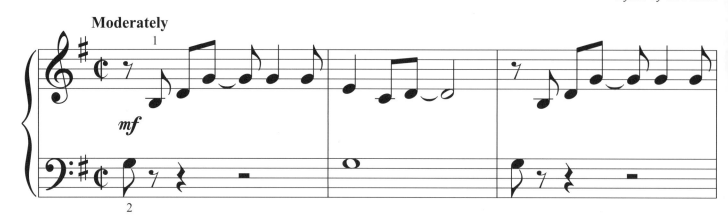

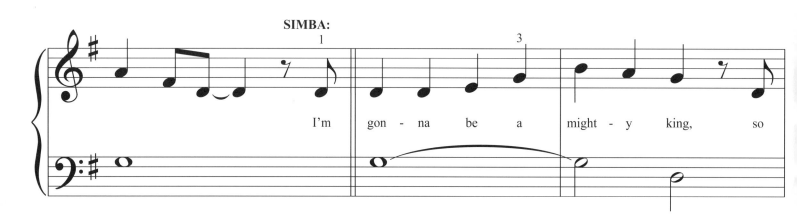

SIMBA:

I'm gon - na be a might - y king, so

ZAZU:

en - e - mies be - ware! Well, I've nev - er seen a king of beasts with

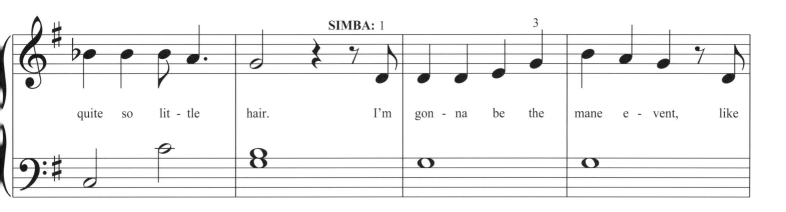

quite so lit - tle hair. I'm gon - na be the mane e - vent, like

no king was be - fore. I'm brush - ing up on look - ing down. I'm

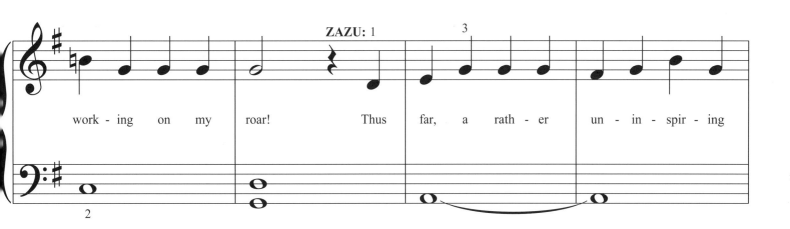

work - ing on my roar! Thus far, a rath - er un - in - spir - ing

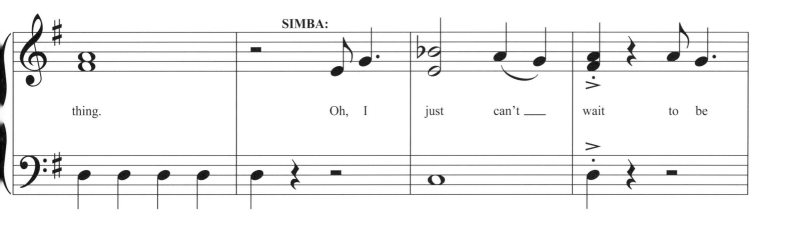

thing. Oh, I just can't ___ wait to be

king! **ZAZU:** *(Spoken) You've* | *rather a long way to go,* | *young master! If you think...*

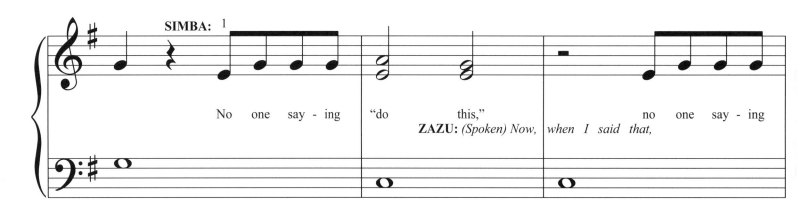

SIMBA: No one say - ing "do this," **ZAZU:** *(Spoken) Now, when I said that,* no one say - ing

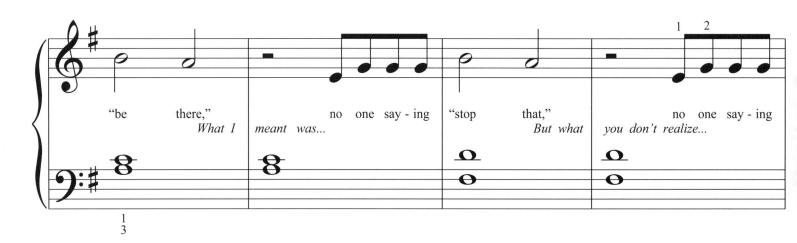

"be there," *What I meant was...* no one say - ing "stop that," *But what you don't realize...* no one say - ing

"see here." ___ *Now see here!* Free to run a - round all ___

day, *Well, that's definitely out.* free to do it all my ___

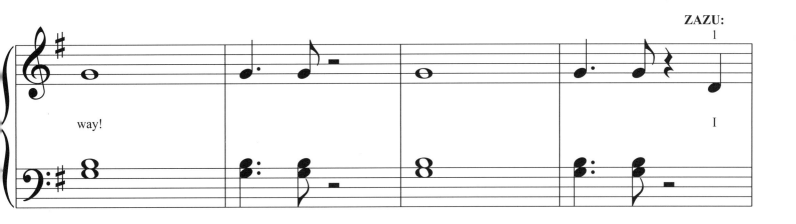

way! I

think it's time that you and I ar - ranged a heart - to - heart.

SIMBA: **ZAZU:**

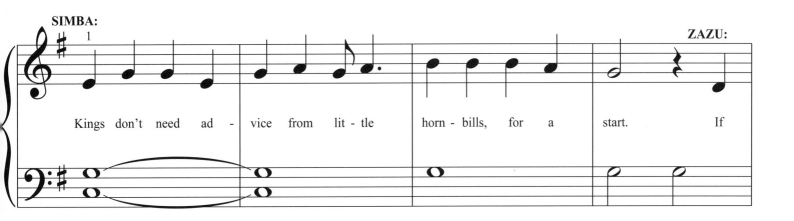

Kings don't need ad - vice from lit - tle horn - bills, for a start. If

42

this is where the mon - ar - chy is head - ed, count me out! Out of

ser - vice, out of Af - ri - ca. ___ I would - n't hang a - bout. This

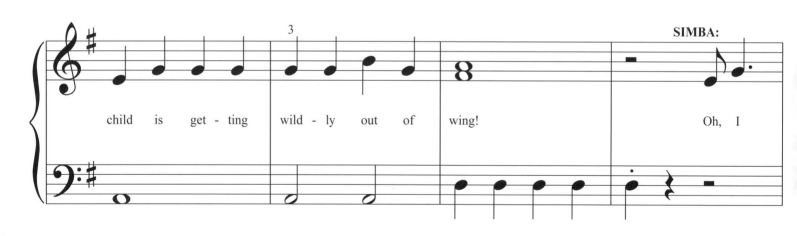

child is get - ting wild - ly out of wing! SIMBA: Oh, I

just can't ___ wait to be king! Ev -'ry - bod - y

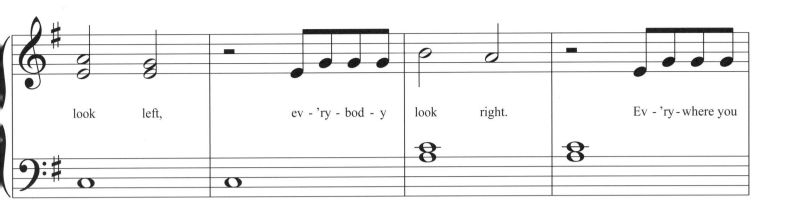

look left,   ev - 'ry - bod - y   look   right.   Ev - 'ry - where you

SIMBA & CHORUS:

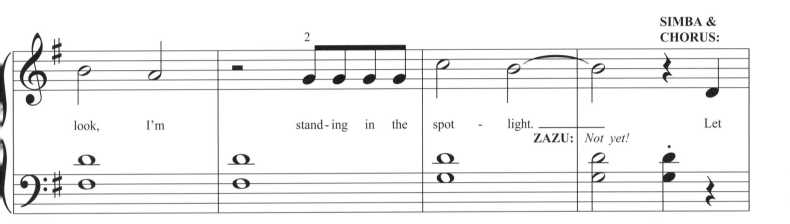

look,   I'm   stand - ing in the spot - light.   Let

ZAZU: *Not yet!*

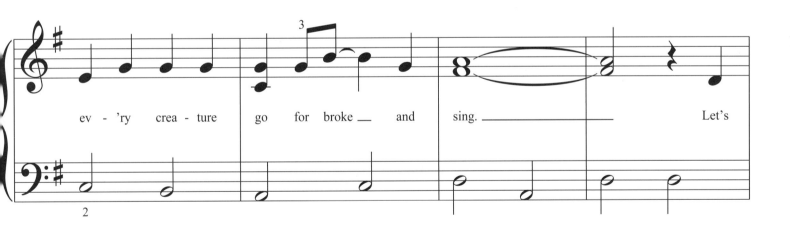

ev - 'ry crea - ture   go for broke and   sing.   Let's

hear it in the   herd and on   the   wing.   It's

SIMBA:

gon - na be King Sim - ba's fin - est fling. Oh, I

just can't ___ wait to be king! Oh, I

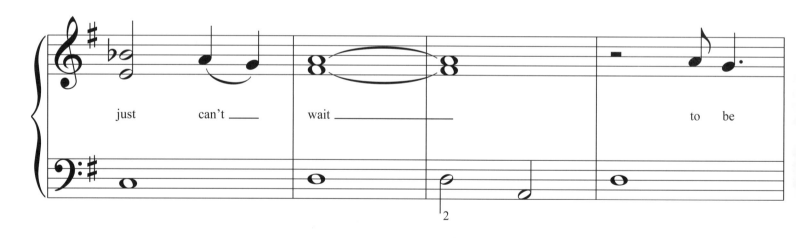

just can't ___ wait ___ to be

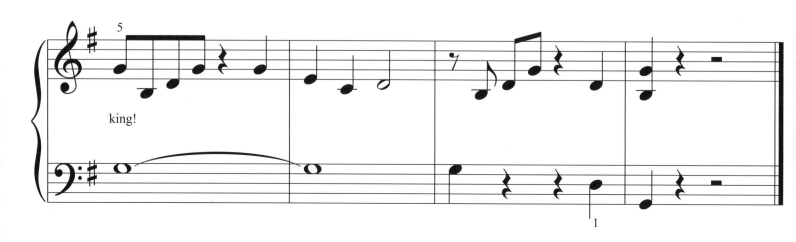

king!

RAFIKI'S FIREFLIES

Composed by
HANS ZIMMER

46

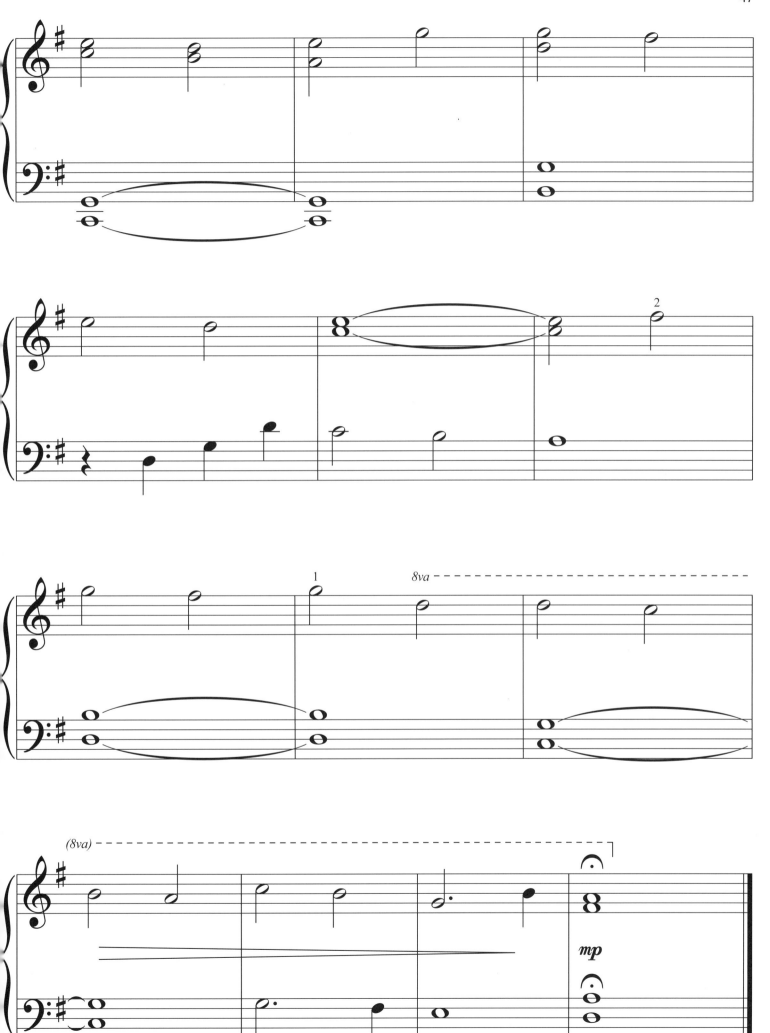

THE LION SLEEPS TONIGHT

New Lyrics and Revised Music by GEORGE DAVID WEISS,
HUGO PERETTI and LUIGI CREATORE

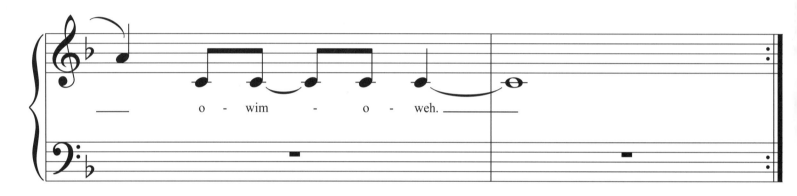

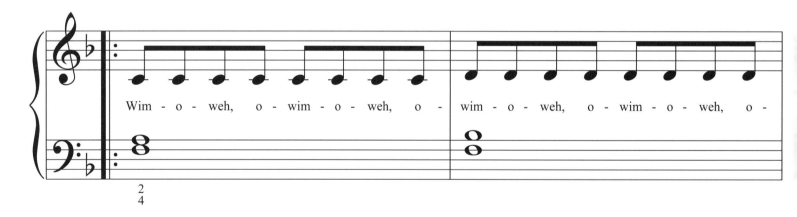

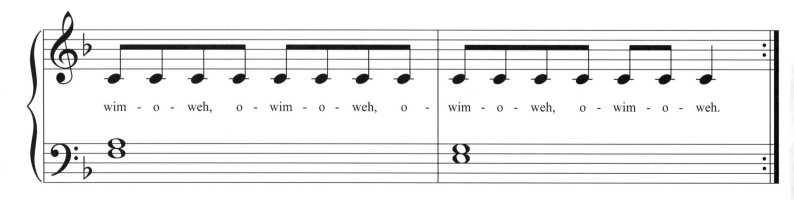

To Coda ⊕

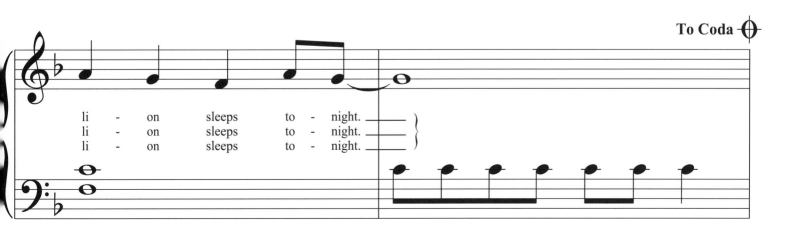

Wee _____ o - wim - o - weh.

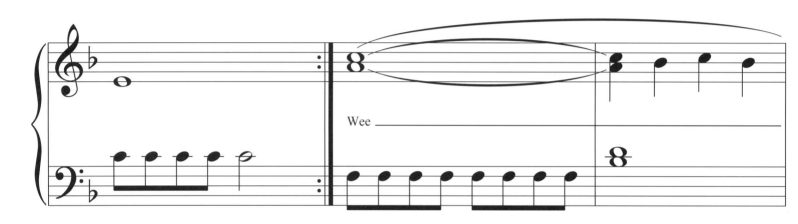

Wee _____

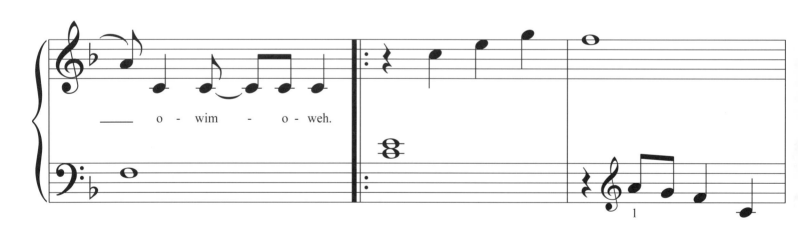

_____ o - wim - o - weh.

D.S. al Coda

8va -

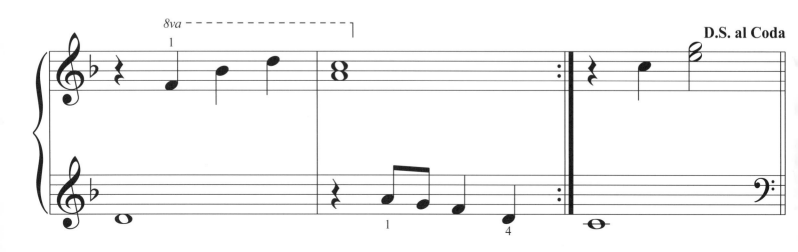

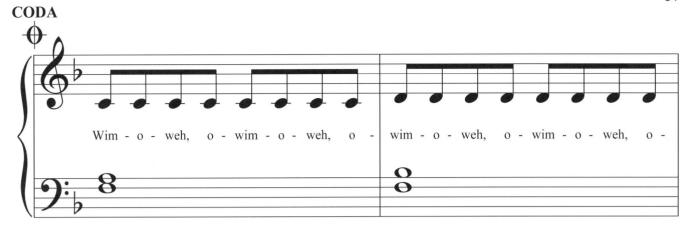

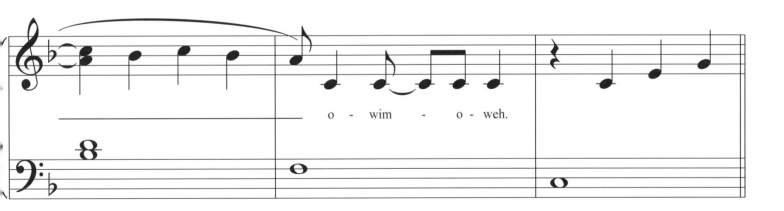

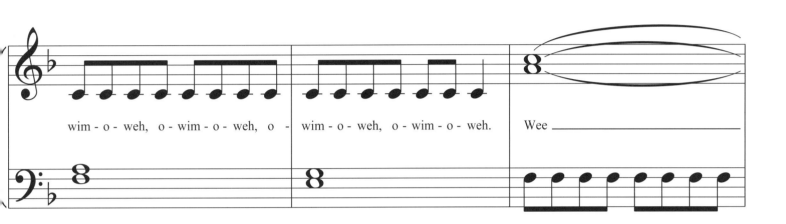

NEVER TOO LATE

Music by ELTON JOHN
Lyrics by TIM RICE

Moderately fast

It's nev-er too late to turn things a-round, ___ but come and un-rav - el the path ___ to con-found. ___ The doubt-ers and los - ers, that line ___

of de - spair, ___ would tell you it's o - ver, you're go - ing no - where. It's

nev - er too late, I hope, ___ it's nev - er too late. ___

It's nev - er too late   to get   back on   track, ___   to
nev - er too late   to get up   off the   ground. _   Don't

get at least some, ___ if not all ___ of it back. ___   I   thought I was hap - py,   and
have to be no - ticed, don't have ___ to be crowned. _   I   did what I've done, _ and   I

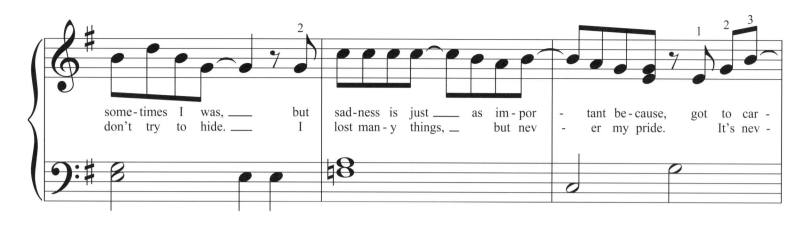

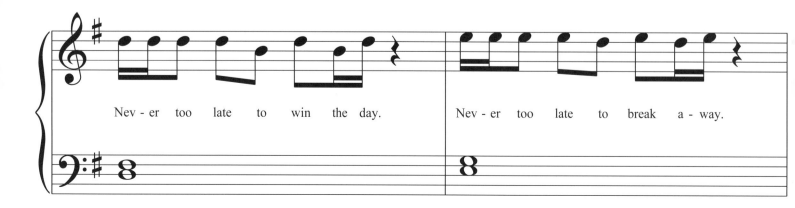

Time is not to move too fast, but time is not my friend. I'm a long way from the start, but

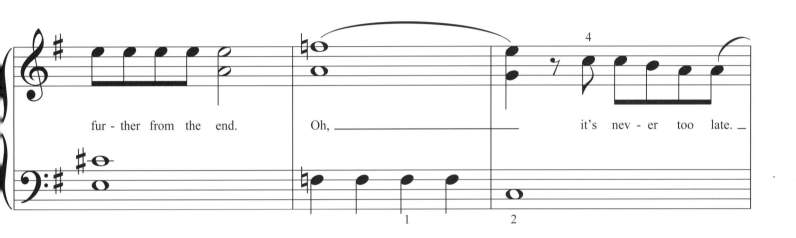

fur - ther from the end. Oh, _____ it's nev - er too late. _

1.

It's

2.

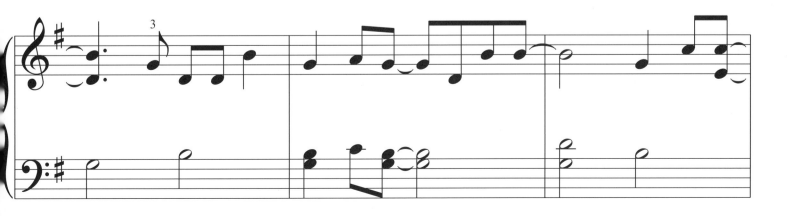

56

used to say, "I don't have time, I'm sleep-ing to-night." __ A day do-in' noth-in' is

do-in' it right. __ No hur-ry, no hur-ry, it takes as long as it takes. You

might as well sleep for all the dif-f'rence it makes. "I did-n't find love or the

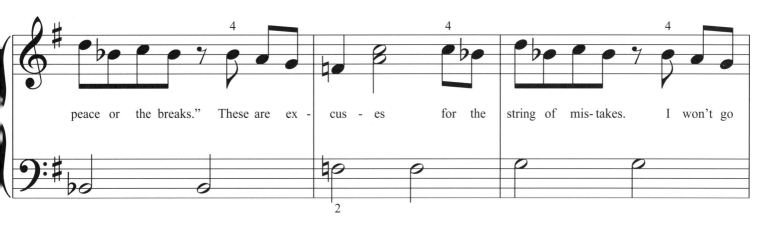

peace or the breaks." These are ex - cus - es   for the   string of mis-takes.   I won't go

back there.   Not go - ing   back   there.

Nev-er too late to fight the fight.   Nev-er too late to cheat the night.

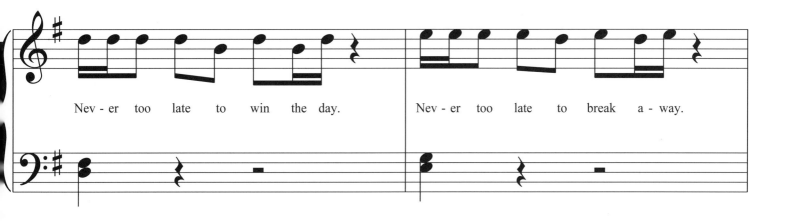

Nev - er too late to win the day.   Nev - er too late to break a - way.

Nev - er too late to fight the fight. Nev - er too late to cheat the night.

Nev - er too late to win the day. Nev - er too late to break a - way.

Time is not to move too fast, but time is not my friend. I'm a long way from the start, but

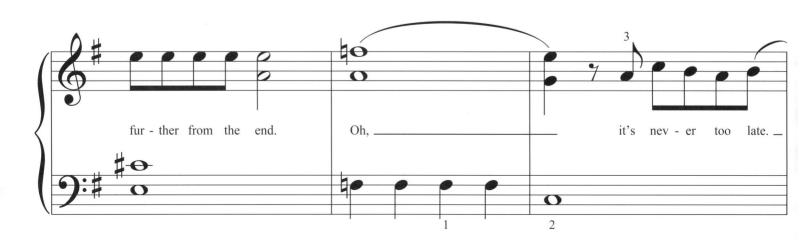

fur - ther from the end. Oh, _____ it's nev - er too late. _

REMEMBER

Composed by HANS ZIMMER
"CIRCLE OF LIFE"
Music by ELTON JOHN
Lyrics by TIM RICE

Slowly

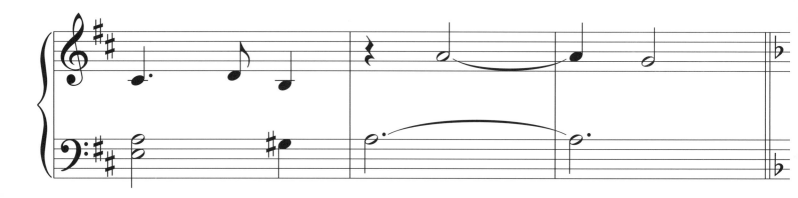

Slightly faster

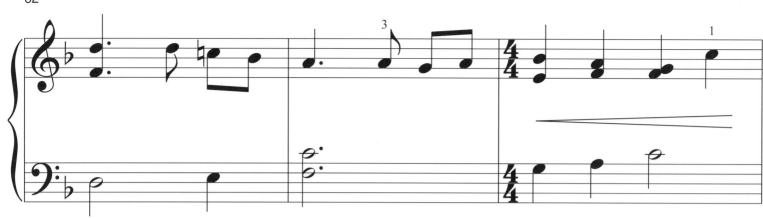

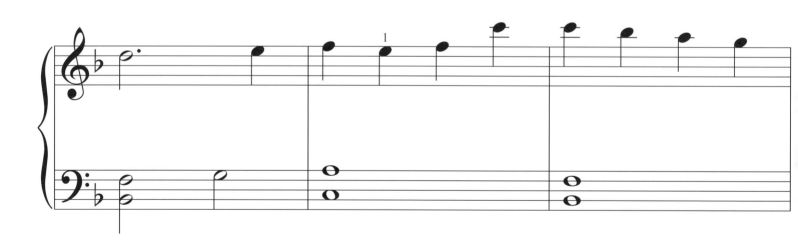

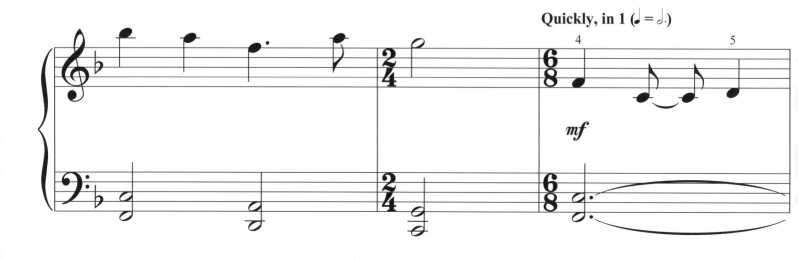

Moderately

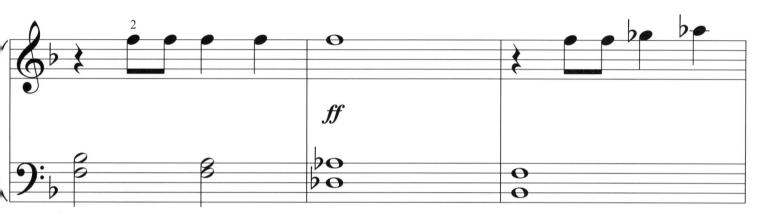

SIMBA IS ALIVE!

Composed by
HANS ZIMMER

SPIRIT

Written by TIMOTHY McKENZIE,
ILYA SALMANZADEH and BEYONCÉ

sky, yeah. Watch the light lift your heart up, burn your flame through the
sky, yeah. Let the light lift your heart up, burn your flame through the

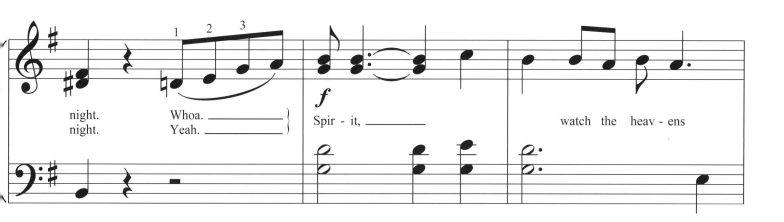

night. Whoa. Spir - it, watch the heav - ens
night. Yeah.

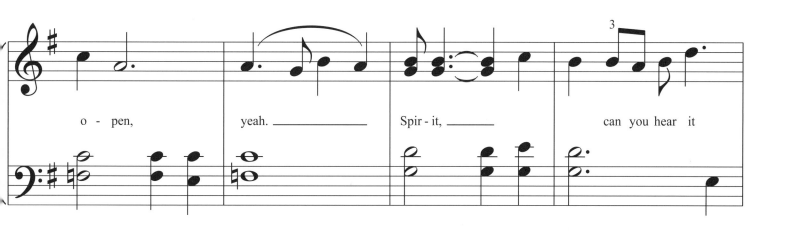

o - pen, yeah. Spir - it, can you hear it

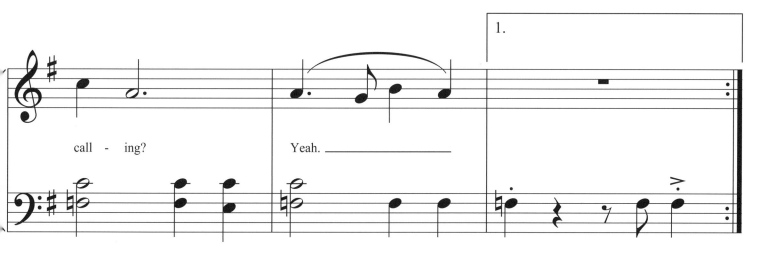

1.

call - ing? Yeah.

Your des - ti - ny is com - ing close; stand up and fight. _____

_____ So, go _____ in - to that far _____ off _____ land _____ and be _____

_____ one with the great I _____ Am, I Am. _____ Boy _____ be -

comes _____ a _____ man. _____ Whoa. _____ Spir - it, _____

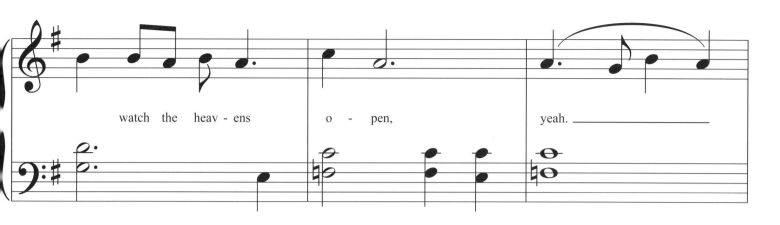

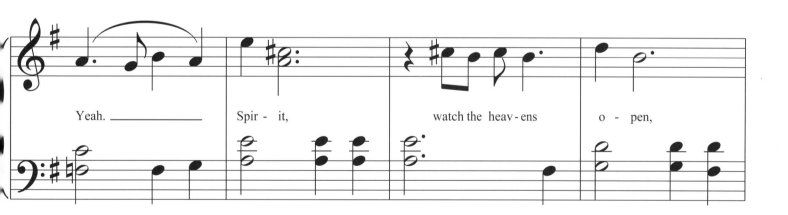

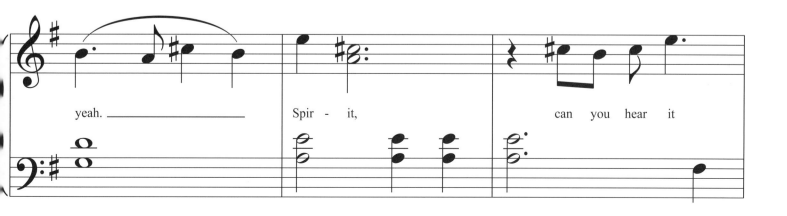

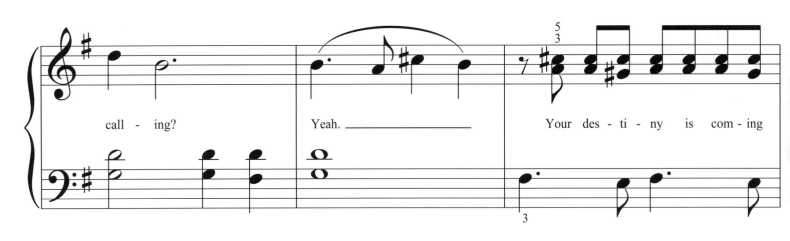

calling?   Yeah. _____   Your des - ti - ny is com - ing

close;   stand up and   fight. _____   So, go ___

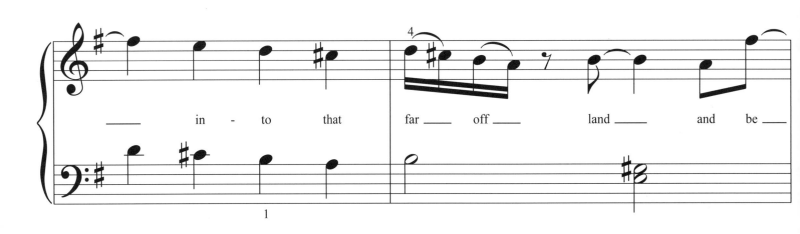

___ in - to that   far ___ off ___ land ___ and be ___

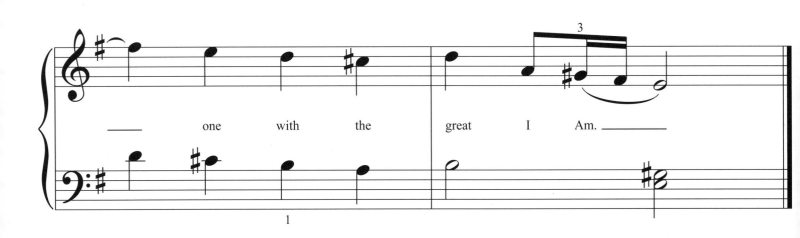

___ one with the   great I Am. _____